THE BEST WAY TO LIVE AND DIE

THE BEST
WAY
TO LIVE AND DIE

DONALD W. FLOOD

Copyright © Donald W. Flood, 1999

All rights reserved.

ISBN:

978-0-473-52414-2 (Softcover)

978-0-473-52416-6 (Kindle)

978-0-473-52415-9 (EPUB)

978-0-473-52417-3 (Audiobook)

A catalogue record for this book is available from the
National Library of New Zealand

Also available as an audiobook from

Islamic Audiobooks Central

https://islamicaudiobookscentral.com

CONTENTS

I GATHERING THE INITIAL PIECES OF "THE PURPOSE OF LIFE PUZZLE"

I once thought my upbringing offered an excellent way of life, especially since I felt satisfied — both mentally and physically. As a young man, I lived the life of an average American who had a rather hedonistic lifestyle; I was fond of music, a festive atmosphere, women, sports, travel, ethnic foods and foreign languages. I reached a point, however, where I felt 'spiritually bankrupt' and I asked myself, "now what?" and I thought, "there has to be more to life than this." This realization was the impetus that led me to search for the truth through diverse avenues..

I assumed the reason I felt spiritually unfulfilled had to do with my lifestyle in America, which was often tied to instant gratification and impulsive behavior. As a result, I speculated that the answer might lie in finding a better locale. Thus, I began looking for that perfect place. After traveling to numerous destinations, I discovered that it wasn't so much a perfect location I was looking for, but a particular culture with the most suitable approach to life. When I found what I considered to be the most appealing culture, I recognized that it still had flaws. Thereafter, I surmised that we should learn about the different ways people live and then select the best from these practices. This was perhaps what set me on my journey to seek the truth.

Unable to really implement the life of a global citizen, I chose to read materials on metaphysics because the esoteric things in life always intrigued me. I quickly learned everything functions according to universal laws which can be used for one's own benefit. After reading many books on this subject, I concluded that more important than these laws is the One Who created them, that is, God. I also discovered metaphysics can be a precarious path to follow, in which case, I refrained from any further readings in this area.

On the suggestion of a good friend, we went on a three-month camping trip all over America and Western Canada with the intention of discovering the purpose of life. We witnessed the marvels of nature and realized this world could not have been created by mistake, and that it was clearly a wonderland of signs pointing to its Creator. Hence, this trip reinforced my belief in God.

After returning home, I felt distressed at the busy life of the city, so I turned to meditation for relief. I was able to find inner peace through meditation techniques. Nevertheless, this tranquil feeling was only temporary; once I stood up, I couldn't take that feeling with me.

Likewise, being consistent with meditation became too much of a formidable task, so I slowly started losing interest.

Before long, I thought the truth might lie in self-improvement. Therefore, I became a voracious reader of motivational materials and attended related seminars. In addition, I was striving to live up to the US Army's slogan on TV commercials, *'Be all you can be'*, through endeavors in fire-walking, skydiving and martial arts. Due to my reading and challenging exploits, I gained a keen sense of self-confidence, but in fact, I still hadn't discovered the truth.

Soon afterwards, I read numerous books on various philosophies. I found many interesting concepts and practices; yet, there wasn't any particular philosophy that I could totally agree with. Thus, I chose to consolidate what I thought was the best wisdom from among these doctrines. It became sort of a *'religion à la carte'* which mainly emphasized good moral behavior. I eventually concluded that good morality was good, but it was not good enough to solve 'the purpose of life puzzle' which was a more spiritual approach to life.

Shortly thereafter, I obtained a job in a Muslim country where I had enough of free time to read and reflect on life. While continuing my search for the truth, I found a recommendation in a book concerning the need for sincere repentance to God. I proceeded to do so and felt remorse for all the people I had wronged in my life, to the degree that tears started rolling down my face.

A few days later, I had a conversation with some Muslim friends. I mentioned to them that I was used to having a lot more freedom in America than what was present in their country. One person said,

"Well, it depends on what you mean by *'freedom'*. In your part of the world, no matter how well parents teach morality to their children inside the home, as soon as they go outside, they generally encounter the society in contradiction to that morality. On the other hand, in most Muslim communities, the morals taught to the children at home are very similar to what they find away from home. So who really has the freedom here?"

From this analogy, I inferred that the Islamic guidelines and restrictions partially sanctioning human behavior are not meant to curtail human freedom;

rather, they served to define and dignify human freedom.

A further opportunity to learn about Islam arose when I was invited to sit with a group of Muslims over dinner. After mentioning to the group that I had been living in Las Vegas, Nevada before coming to the Middle East, a Muslim from America said,

"You must make sure you die as a good Muslim."

I immediately asked him to explain what he meant. He said,

"If you die as a non-Muslim, it is like

playing the game of roulette in which you put all of your chips (all of your life, including your deeds and your particular belief in God) on only one number, just hoping that perhaps by the Mercy of God, you will enter Paradise on Judgment Day. In contrast, if you die as a good Muslim, it is like spreading your chips all over the roulette board, so that every number is covered. In this way, no matter what number the ball falls on, you're safe. In other words, living and dying as a good Muslim is the best insurance you will not go to the Hell, and at the same time, it is the best investment that you'll go to Paradise."

As a former resident of Las Vegas, I could directly relate to this poignant example with the game of roulette.

At this point, I understood I would not find the truth until I established a relationship with God. That being the case, I decided to concentrate on those religions in which God had sent revelation to His prophets and messengers. Hence, I chose to continue my search for the truth through Christianity and Islam.

II CHRISTIANITY IN FOCUS

Even though I grew up as a Christian, I had been confused and uninterested in Christianity. I felt like I inherited a mysterious religion beyond understanding. I believe it was for this reason that I was a Christian by name but not in practice. Furthermore, I realized my doubt about Christian beliefs caused me to be in a state of non-religiousness. Nonetheless, while I was searching for the truth, I had a chance to re-examine those beliefs I inherited from my parents yet never bothered to scrutinize.

Through booklets, cassettes and videotapes on Christianity produced by Muslims and non-Muslims, I surprisingly found out about hundreds of verses in the Bible which reveal a lack of harmony in Christian beliefs. According to these materials, God was

One prior to Jesus (peace be upon him). Likewise, Jesus propagated the belief in One God. However, after Jesus, Christianity emphasized the Trinity instead of the Oneness of God. Also, before Jesus, God was without sons and equals. Similarly, Jesus said he was God's Messenger, whereas after his time, Christianity stressed that Jesus is God's son or God Himself.

Regarding monotheism, the first of the Ten Commandments upholds Jesus' assertion for the belief in One God,

"...Hear, O Israel, the Lord our God is one Lord." (Mark 12:29)

Likewise, there is plethora of verses in the Bible that refute the divinity of Jesus (peace be upon him). For example, Jesus admitted he could not do miracles independently, but only by the Will and permission of God. Interestingly, it says in the Bible that Jesus prayed. I asked myself, "How can Jesus be God and pray to God at the same time?" A praying God is a contradiction.

Additionally, Jesus states that his teachings are not his own, but those of the One who sent him. Logically, if what he says is not his own, he is just a prophet receiving revelation from God like those before (and after) him.

Moreover, Jesus admits that he does what he is taught by God. Again, I asked myself, "How can Jesus be taught and be God at the same time?" In my discussions with Muslims, they concurred with what Jesus commanded with respect to the belief in only One God, as in the following Qur'anic verse:

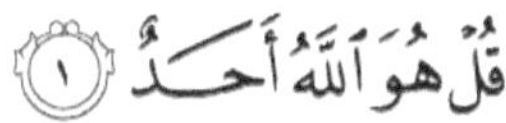

"Say: "He is God, [Who is] One."

(Qur'aan 112:1)

I was also surprised to find out about the verses in the Bible which refer to Jesus as a prophet of God. Likewise, I learned about the Islamic view of Jesus which is that he is a prophet and messenger of God. In the Qur'aan, God says,

مَّا ٱلْمَسِيحُ ٱبْنُ مَرْيَمَ إِلَّا رَسُولٌ قَدْ خَلَتْ مِن قَبْلِهِ ٱلرُّسُلُ وَأُمُّهُۥ صِدِّيقَةٌ ۖ كَانَا يَأْكُلَانِ ٱلطَّعَامَ ٱنظُرْ كَيْفَ نُبَيِّنُ لَهُمُ ٱلْآيَاتِ ثُمَّ ٱنظُرْ أَنَّىٰ يُؤْفَكُونَ ۝

"The Messiah, son of Mary, is not but a messenger; [other] messengers have passed on before him. And his mother was a supporter of truth. They both used to eat food. Look how We make clear to them the signs; then look how they are deluded."

(Qur'aan 5:75)

Another common belief in

Christianity is that Jesus is the son of God.

According to the Bible, it was customary to call any prophet of God, or righteous man, a son of God. Jesus called himself the son of man, not God or God's literal son. Evidently, Paul was most responsible for elevating the status of Jesus to the son of God, distorting the teachings of Jesus (peace be upon him).

What's more, Jesus did not appear to be the 'begotten' son of God (as it used to say in John 3:16) since this word has been canceled from the Revised Standard Version (RSV), as well as many other new versions of the Bible. Furthermore, God emphatically says in the Qur'aan that He does not have a son. However, God also declared that He created Adam and Jesus:

إِنَّ مَثَلَ عِيسَىٰ عِندَ ٱللَّهِ كَمَثَلِ ءَادَمَ خَلَقَهُۥ مِن تُرَابٍ ثُمَّ قَالَ لَهُۥ كُن فَيَكُونُ ﴿٥٩﴾

"Indeed, the example of Jesus to God is like that of Adam. He created him from dust; then He said to him "Be", and he was."

(Qur'aan 3:59)

Subsequent to these modifications, emperors and clergy made further fabrications, contrary to what Jesus said or did. Of these is the concept of Trinity, in which Jesus is one of the three manifestations of the Trinitarian God: the Father, the Son and the Holy Ghost (See: 1 John 5:7). In the Bible, this verse given as the best proof for the Doctrine of Trinity, even though this doctrine was never put forth by Jesus, his disciples, or early Christian scholars. In fact, it was enacted only after much disagreement and conflict among Christians in the year 325 AD at the Council of Nicea. Interestingly, this verse has been expunged from the Bibles of the modern age.

In addition, the Qur'aan warns the

Jews and Christians to refrain from disbelieving in the revelation of God and against believing in Trinity.

A related area of controversy I read about was the *'original sin'* and salvation through *'the crucifixion'* of Jesus. Presumably, before Jesus, there was no Doctrine of Original Sin. However, after Jesus, the Doctrine of Original Sin appeared. Moreover, before Jesus, salvation was obtained by obedience to God whereas after Jesus, salvation was achieved through his crucifixion — so they said.

In Christianity, the Doctrine of

Original Sin is the justification for having salvation through the crucifixion of Jesus. Nevertheless, I found out that this doctrine is strongly negated in the Old Testament. It seems this concept may have been designed as a way for its believers to eschew their accountability of sins before God on Judgment Day. It was brought to my attention that, according to Jesus, man is saved through obedience and submission to God. Correspondingly, in the Qur'aan, every soul is compensated for what it earns. However, it seems that this doctrine was changed, making salvation through the crucifixion of Jesus (peace be upon him).

The theory of salvation through crucifixion holds that Jesus offered himself willingly to be crucified to ransom and save humanity. If so, why did Jesus request the help from God before the soldiers came to arrest him?

"...Father, save me from this hour." (John 12:27)

Likewise, why does the Bible say Jesus cried out in a loud voice beseeching God for help on the cross:

"...My God, my God, why have you forsaken me?" (Matthew 27:46)

In addition, how could Jesus have been crucified for the salvation of all humans when he was sent only to the Children of Israel? This is clearly a contradiction. I found the foregoing verses to be very convincing that Jesus was not crucified on the cross to redeem the sins of mankind.

The Qur'aan says they did not kill or crucify him, but it was someone else who was made to look like him. If this is the case, then it may explain the appearance of Jesus to his disciples after the crucifixion. If he had really died on the cross, then he would have come to his disciples in a spiritual body. As shown in Luke 24:36-43, Jesus met them with his physical body after the event of his alleged crucifixion. Accordingly, I learned it was Paul who taught the resurrection of Jesus. Paul also admitted the resurrection was his own gospel.

I came across many sources indicating that Paul and others were frustrated by the Jewish rejection of the message of Jesus, so they extended their call to the Gentiles. They reached into southern Europe, where polytheism and idolatry were spreading. Gradually, the message of Jesus was modified to suit the tastes and traditions of the Romans and

Greeks of those days. The Bible warns against adding or removing information from its teachings, which is precisely what happened. God addresses this point in the Qur'aan as well,

فَوَيْلٌ لِّلَّذِينَ يَكْتُبُونَ ٱلْكِتَبَ بِأَيْدِيهِمْ ثُمَّ يَقُولُونَ هَٰذَا مِنْ عِندِ ٱللَّهِ لِيَشْتَرُواْ بِهِۦ ثَمَنًا قَلِيلًا ۖ فَوَيْلٌ لَّهُم مِّمَّا كَتَبَتْ أَيْدِيهِمْ وَوَيْلٌ لَّهُم مِّمَّا يَكْسِبُونَ ﴿٧٩﴾

"So woe to those who write the "scripture" with their own hands, then say, "This is from God," in order to exchange it for a small price. Woe to them for what their hands have written, and woe to them for what they earn."

(Qur'aan 2:79)

III PROPHET MUHAMMAD IN THE SCRIPTURES

Another interesting point I learned about concerns Biblical prophecies on the advent of Prophet Muhammad (peace be upon him). I discovered that clear prophecies exist in the Bible, even after the original text had been distorted, foretelling the coming of Prophet Muhammad after Jesus. Muslim scholars have affirmed that the description by Jesus of the one to come after him cannot apply to any other person but Prophet Muhammad. Furthermore, there is a verse in the Holy Qur'aan confirming what Jesus said regarding this point,

وَإِذْ قَالَ عِيسَى ابْنُ مَرْيَمَ يَٰبَنِىٓ إِسْرَٰٓءِيلَ إِنِّى رَسُولُ ٱللَّهِ إِلَيْكُم مُّصَدِّقًا لِّمَا بَيْنَ يَدَىَّ مِنَ ٱلتَّوْرَىٰةِ وَمُبَشِّرًۢا بِرَسُولٍ يَأْتِى مِنۢ بَعْدِى ٱسْمُهُۥٓ أَحْمَدُ فَلَمَّا جَآءَهُم بِٱلْبَيِّنَٰتِ قَالُوا۟ هَٰذَا سِحْرٌ مُّبِينٌ ﴿٦﴾

"... O Children of Israel, I am the Messenger of God to you confirming what came before me of the Torah and bringing good tidings of a Messenger to come after me, whose name is Ahmad..."

(Qur'aan 61:6)

The name Ahmad is another name for Prophet Muhammad and is derived from the same root word.

IV PROPHET MUHAMMAD IN THE QUR'AAN

I observed that the Qur'aan directs us to believe in God and Prophet Muhammad as in the following verse:

قُل يَـٰٓأَيُّهَا ٱلنَّاسُ إِنِّي رَسُولُ ٱللَّهِ إِلَيۡكُمۡ جَمِيعًا ٱلَّذِى لَهُۥ مُلۡكُ ٱلسَّمَـٰوَٰتِ وَٱلۡأَرۡضِ لَآ إِلَـٰهَ إِلَّا هُوَ يُحۡيِۦ وَيُمِيتُ فَـَٔامِنُوا۟ بِٱللَّهِ وَرَسُولِهِ ٱلنَّبِيِّ ٱلۡأُمِّيِّ ٱلَّذِى يُؤۡمِنُ بِٱللَّهِ وَكَلِمَـٰتِهِۦ وَٱتَّبِعُوهُ لَعَلَّكُمۡ تَهۡتَدُونَ ۝

"Say, [O Muhammad]: 'O mankind, Indeed, I am the Messenger of God to you all — from Him to Whom belongs the dominion of the heavens and the earth. There is no deity except Him; He gives life and causes death. So believe in God and His Messenger, the illiterate prophet, who believes in God and His words, and follow him that you may be guided.'"

(Qur'aan 7:158)

I came to know that the Qur'aan also

refers to Prophet Muhammad, peace be upon him, as the last prophet:

مَّا كَانَ مُحَمَّدٌ أَبَآ أَحَدٍ مِّن رِّجَالِكُمْ وَلَكِن رَّسُولَ ٱللَّهِ وَخَاتَمَ ٱلنَّبِيِّـنَ وَكَانَ ٱللَّهُ بِكُلِّ شَيْءٍ عَلِيمًا ﴿٤٠﴾

"Muhammad is not the father of any of your men, but he is the Messenger of God and the seal of the prophets..."

(Qur'aan 33:40)

Even though God states in the Qur'aan that Muhammad is the last prophet, I discovered that Muslims still believe in and accept all the previous prophets, along with the revelations they received in their *original* form.

V THE QUR'AAN: THE LAST REVELATION

I comprehended that it was fundamentally due to innovations attributed to divine revelation that the need arose for another prophet after

Jesus with another revelation after the Gospel. This is why God sent Muhammad, peace be upon him, with the last Message, that is, the Qur'aan, to bring all of mankind back to the belief in and worship of One God, without partners or intermediaries. According to the Muslims, the Holy Qur'aan is the permanent and ultimate source of guidance for mankind. It offers a rational and historical elucidation of the magnificent role of Jesus. The name Jesus is cited twenty-five times in the Qur'aan, which also contains a chapter called Maryam (Mary), named after the mother of Jesus, peace be upon him.

Regarding the divine authenticity of this last revelation, I found the following Qur'anic verses very compelling:

وَمَا كَانَ هَٰذَا ٱلْقُرْءَانُ أَن يُفْتَرَىٰ مِن دُونِ ٱللَّهِ وَلَٰكِن تَصْدِيقَ ٱلَّذِى بَيْنَ يَدَيْهِ وَتَفْصِيلَ ٱلْكِتَٰبِ لَا رَيْبَ فِيهِ مِن رَّبِّ ٱلْعَٰلَمِينَ ﴿٣٧﴾

"It was not possible for this Qur'aan to be produced by other than God, but it is a confirmation of what was before it and a detailed explanation of the former Scripture, about which there is no doubt, from the Lord of the worlds."

(Qur'aan 10:37)

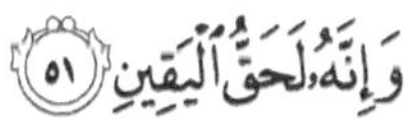

"Indeed, it is the truth of certainty."

(Qur'aan 69:51)

Similarly, I was concerned about the adulteration of the Qur'aan since this was a major problem with the previous revelations. I read that the Qur'aan will never change or be abrogated:

إِنَّا نَحْنُ نَزَّلْنَا ٱلذِّكْرَ وَإِنَّا لَهُ لَحَفِظُونَ ﴿٩﴾

"Indeed, it is We who sent down the Message and indeed, We will be its guardian."

(Qur'aan 15:9)

I was also informed about some of the scientific phenomena mentioned in the Qur'aan, which give credence to the belief that the Qur'aan is the literal word of God. There are verses describing human embryonic development, mountains, the origin of the universe, the cerebrum, seas, deep seas, and internal waves and clouds. It is beyond explanation that anyone, more than fourteen hundred years ago, could have known these facts, which were found or confirmed only recently by advanced mechanisms and sophisticated scientific procedures.

VI ISLAM: THE ESSENCE AND CULMINATION OF REVEALED RELIGIONS

Muslims believe that the essential purpose for which mankind was created is the worship of

God. As He said in the Qur'aan,

$$وَمَا خَلَقْتُ ٱلْجِنَّ وَٱلْإِنسَ إِلَّا لِيَعْبُدُونِ ﴿٥٦﴾$$

"I did not create the jinn and mankind except to worship Me."

(Qur'aan 51:56)

Related to this, a well known Islamic scholar from the West says,

"The most complete system of worship available to humans today is the system found in the religion of Islam. The very name 'Islam' means 'submission to the Will of God'. Although it commonly is referred to as 'the third of the three monotheistic faiths', it is not a new religion at all. It is the religion brought by all the prophets of God for humankind. Islam was the religion of Adam, Abraham, Moses and Jesus."

In addition he states,

"Since there is only one God, and humankind is one species, the religion that God has ordained for humans is essentially one... Human spiritual and social needs are uniform and human nature has not changed since the first man and woman were created."

(End of quote from: *The Purpose of Creation*, by Dr. Bilal Philips)

Uncovering the fact that the message of God has always been the same, I realized it is the duty of all human beings to seek the truth and not just blindly accept the religion that their society or parents follow. According to the Qur'aan,

مَا تَعْبُدُونَ مِن دُونِهِ إِلَّا أَسْمَاءً سَمَّيْتُمُوهَا أَنتُمْ وَءَابَآؤُكُم مَّا أَنزَلَ ٱللَّهُ بِهَا مِن سُلْطَٰنٍ إِنِ ٱلْحُكْمُ إِلَّا لِلَّهِ أَمَرَ أَلَّا تَعْبُدُوٓا۟ إِلَّآ إِيَّاهُ ذَٰلِكَ ٱلدِّينُ ٱلْقَيِّمُ وَلَٰكِنَّ أَكْثَرَ ٱلنَّاسِ لَا يَعْلَمُونَ ﴿٤٠﴾

"You worship besides Him mere names you have forged, you and your fathers, for which God has sent down no authority..."

(Qur'aan 12:40)

Regarding *fitrah*, that is, the inherent nature of man to worship God prior to the corruption of his nature by external influences, Prophet Muhammad (peace be upon him) said,

"Every child is born on the *fitrah* and his parents convert him to Judaism, Christianity or Magianism. As an animal delivers a perfect baby animal — do you find it mutilated?"

Furthermore, God says,

فَأَقِمْ وَجْهَكَ لِلدِّينِ حَنِيفًا فِطْرَتَ ٱللَّهِ ٱلَّتِي فَطَرَ ٱلنَّاسَ عَلَيْهَا لَا تَبْدِيلَ لِخَلْقِ ٱللَّهِ ذَٰلِكَ ٱلدِّينُ ٱلْقَيِّمُ وَلَٰكِنَّ أَكْثَرَ ٱلنَّاسِ لَا يَعْلَمُونَ ﴿٣٠﴾

"So direct yourself to the religion

inclining toward truth — the *fitrah* of God upon which He has created [all] people. No change should there be in the creation of God. That is the correct religion, but most of the people do not know."

(Qur'aan 30:30)

Moreover, I learned there is no other religion acceptable to God besides Islam, as He clearly states in the Qur'aan:

وَمَن يَبْتَغِ غَيْرَ ٱلْإِسْلَٰمِ دِينًا فَلَن يُقْبَلَ مِنْهُ وَهُوَ فِى ٱلْأَخِرَةِ مِنَ ٱلْخَٰسِرِينَ ۝

"Whoever desires other than Islam as a religion, never will it be accepted from him, and he, in the Hereafter, will be among the losers."

(Qur'aan 3:85)

I deduced that man might neglect the guidance of God and establish his own standards of living. Ultimately, however, he will discover it is only a mirage that eluded him.

VII A TRAVELER

As I continued to read the Qur'aan and learn about the sayings and doings of Prophet Muhammad [the Sunnah], I noticed Islam views man as a traveler in this life and that 'Home' is in the next life for eternity! We are here for a short period and we cannot take anything with us from this life except our belief in God and our deeds. Thus, man should be like a traveler who passes through the land and does not become attached to it.

As travelers on this journey, we must understand that the meaning of being alive is to be tested. Hence, there is suffering, joy, pain and elation. These tests of good and evil are intended to evoke our higher spiritual qualities. Yet, we are incapable of benefiting from these tests unless we do our best, have complete trust in God and patiently accept what He has destined for us.

VIII THE ROAD TO PARADISE

It was very meaningful to me to learn about paradise since this must certainly be the ultimate goal of every individual. Regarding this eternal home, God says,

فَلَا تَعْلَمُ نَفْسٌ مَّا أُخْفِىَ لَهُم مِّن قُرَّةِ أَعْيُنٍ جَزَآءً بِمَا كَانُوا يَعْمَلُونَ ﴿١٧﴾

"No soul knows what has been hidden for it of comfort and satisfaction — as a reward for what it used to do."

(Qur'aan 32:17)

I also became aware of a pleasure that is beyond all imagination, which is to be in the presence of the Creator Himself. I wondered who are the souls worthy of such a reward? This reward of paradise was priceless. I was told the price is true faith, which is proven by obedience to God and following the Sunnah (or way) of Prophet Muhammad (peace be upon him).

I grasped that mankind must worship God to attain righteousness and the spiritual status necessary to enter paradise. This means human beings have to comprehend that worship is as indispensable as eating and breathing — and not a favor they are doing for God. Likewise, I found out that we need to read the Qur'aan to find out what kind of people God wants us to be and then try to become as such. This is the road to paradise.

IX OVERCOMING AN OBSTACLE

At this point, I felt about eighty percent sure I wanted to become a Muslim, but something was holding me back. I was concerned about the reaction of my family and friends if they knew that I had become a Muslim. Shortly thereafter, I expressed this concern to a Muslim who told me that on Judgment Day, no one will be able to help you — not your father, mother or any of your friends. Therefore, if you believe Islam is the true religion, you should embrace it and live your life to please the one who created you. Thus, it became very lucid to me that we are all in the same boat; every soul shall taste death and then we will be liable for our particular belief in God and for our deeds.

X A MEANINGFUL VIDEOTAPE

By this stage in my search for the truth, I was on the verge of embracing Islam. I watched an Islamic lecture on videotape about the purpose of life. The main theme of this lecture was that the purpose of life may be summed up in one word, that is, Islam — peaceful submission to the will of God.

An additional point was that, unlike other religions or beliefs, the term 'Islam' is not associated with any particular person or place. God has *named* the religion in the following Qur'anic verse:

إِنَّ ٱلدِّينَ عِندَ ٱللَّهِ ٱلْإِسْلَٰمُ وَمَا ٱخْتَلَفَ ٱلَّذِينَ أُوتُوا۟ ٱلْكِتَٰبَ إِلَّا مِنۢ بَعْدِ مَا جَآءَهُمُ ٱلْعِلْمُ بَغْيًۢا بَيْنَهُمْ وَمَن يَكْفُرْ بِـَٔايَٰتِ ٱللَّهِ فَإِنَّ ٱللَّهَ سَرِيعُ ٱلْحِسَابِ ﴿١٩﴾

"Indeed, the only religion acceptable

to God is Islam..."

(Qur'aan 3:19)

Anyone who embraces Islam is called a Muslim regardless of that person's race, sex or nationality. This is one of the reasons why Islam is a universal religion.

Prior to my search for the truth, I had never seriously considered Islam as an option because of the constant negative portrayal of Muslims in the media. Similarly, it was disclosed in this videotape that although Islam, is characterized by high moral standards, not all Muslims uphold these standards.

I learned the same can be said about adherents of other religions. I finally understood that we cannot judge a religion by the actions of its followers alone, as I had done, because all humans are fallible. On that account, we should not judge Islam by the actions of its proponents, but by its revelation: the Holy Qur'aan, and the Sunnah of Prophet Muhammad (peace be upon him).

The last point I picked up from this lecture concerned the importance of gratitude. God mentions in the Qur'aan that we should be grateful for the fact that He created us:

وَٱللَّهُ أَخْرَجَكُم مِّنۢ بُطُونِ أُمَّهَٰتِكُمْ لَا تَعْلَمُونَ شَيْـًٔا وَجَعَلَ لَكُمُ ٱلسَّمْعَ وَٱلْأَبْصَٰرَ وَٱلْأَفْـِٔدَةَ لَعَلَّكُمْ تَشْكُرُونَ ﴿٧٨﴾

"God has extracted you from the wombs of your mothers not knowing a thing, and He made for you hearing, vision and hearts that perhaps you would be grateful."

(Qur'aan 16:78)

God has also cited gratitude along with belief, and has made it clear that He gains nothing from punishing His people nor will He gain anything when they give thanks to Him and believe in Him. He says in the Qur'aan,

مَّا يَفْعَلُ ٱللَّهُ بِعَذَابِكُمْ إِن شَكَرْتُمْ وَءَامَنتُمْ وَكَانَ ٱللَّهُ شَاكِرًا عَلِيمًا ﴿١٤٧﴾

"What would God gain from your punishment if you are grateful and believe?"

(Qur'aan 4:147)

XI THE TRUTH UNVEILS ITSELF

As soon as the videotape had finished, I experienced the truth being unveiled to my spirit. I felt a huge burden of sins flying off my back.

Moreover, it felt like my soul was rising above the earth, refusing the makeshift delights of this world in favor of the eternal joys of the Hereafter. This experience, coupled with the long process of reasoning, solved the *'purpose of life puzzle'*. It revealed Islam as the truth, thereby replenishing my *'spiritual landscape'* with belief, purpose, direction and action. I therefore entered the gate of Islam by saying the declaration of faith required to become a Muslim:

Ash-hadu an Laa ilaaha illallaah, wa ash-hadu anna Muhammadan Rasoolullaah.

(I bear witness that there is no true

deity but God and that Muhammad is His Messenger).

I was informed that this formal testimony confirms one's belief in all the prophets and messengers of God, along with all of His divine revelations in their *original* form, thereby updating and completing one's religion to the last of the prophets (Muhammad) and to the final revelation of God (the Qur'aan). The following point became overwhelmingly clear to me: Had Jesus been the last prophet of God and had the Gospel been the final book of revelation, I would have attested to that. As a result, I have naturally chosen to follow the final revelation from the Creator as exemplified by the Seal of the Prophets.

XII IMPRESSIONS OF A NEW MUSLIM

During my search to find the truth, the lesson which transcended all lessons was that all objects of worship other than God are mere delusions. To anyone who sees this clearly, the only possible course is to bring one's own will and actions into complete unison with that of God. Submitting to the will of God has enabled me to feel peace with the Creator, with others and finally, with myself. Consequently, I feel very grateful, that by the Mercy of God, I have been rescued from the depths of ignorance and have stepped into the light of truth.

Islam, the true religion of all times, places and peoples, is a complete code of life which guides man to fulfill the purpose of his existence on earth, and prepares him for the Day when he will return to his Creator. Following this path in a devout manner enables one to gain the pleasure of God and to be closer to Him amid the endless delights of paradise, while escaping from the punishment of hellfire. Another bonus is that our present life will be much happier when we make such a choice.

XIII A DECEPTIVE ENJOYMENT

Embracing Islam has given me more of an insight into the illusive nature of this life. For instance, one basic object of Islam is the liberation of man. This is why a Muslim calls himself 'Abdullaah', the slave of Allaah (that is, God), because enslavement to God signifies liberation from all other forms of servitude, and although modern man may think that he is liberated, he is in fact a slave to his desires. He is generally deceived by this worldly life. He is 'addicted' to hoarding wealth, sex, violence, intoxicants and so on. But above all, he is often seduced by the capitalist system that tends to work through the invention of false needs, which he feels must be satisfied instantly. God says in the Qur'aan,

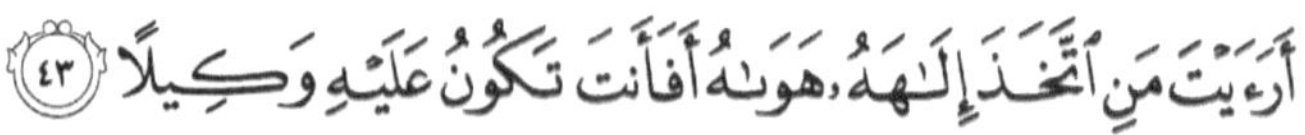

أَمْ تَحْسَبُ أَنَّ أَكْثَرَهُمْ يَسْمَعُونَ أَوْ يَعْقِلُونَ إِنْ هُمْ إِلَّا كَالْأَنْعَامِ بَلْ هُمْ أَضَلُّ سَبِيلًا ۝

"Have you seen the one who takes as his god his own desire? Then would you be responsible for him? Or do you think that most of them hear or reason? They are not except as livestock. Rather, they are even more astray in their way."

(Qur'aan 25:43-44)

Correspondingly, we should not let our zeal to enjoy the pleasures of this fleeting life jeopardize our opportunity to enjoy the bliss of paradise. As God says in the Qur'aan:

زُيِّنَ لِلنَّاسِ حُبُّ ٱلشَّهَوَاتِ مِنَ ٱلنِّسَآءِ وَٱلْبَنِينَ وَٱلْقَنَاطِيرِ ٱلْمُقَنطَرَةِ مِنَ ٱلذَّهَبِ وَٱلْفِضَّةِ وَٱلْخَيْلِ ٱلْمُسَوَّمَةِ وَٱلْأَنْعَامِ وَٱلْحَرْثِ ذَٰلِكَ مَتَاعُ ٱلْحَيَوٰةِ ٱلدُّنْيَا وَٱللَّهُ عِندَهُ حُسْنُ ٱلْمَآبِ ۝ قُلْ أَؤُنَبِّئُكُم بِخَيْرٍ مِّن ذَٰلِكُمْ لِلَّذِينَ ٱتَّقَوْا عِندَ رَبِّهِمْ جَنَّتٌ تَجْرِى مِن تَحْتِهَا ٱلْأَنْهَارُ خَالِدِينَ فِيهَا وَأَزْوَاجٌ مُّطَهَّرَةٌ وَرِضْوَانٌ مِّنَ ٱللَّهِ وَٱللَّهُ بَصِيرٌ بِٱلْعِبَادِ ۝

"Beautified for people is the love of that which they desire—of women, sons, heaped-up sums of gold and silver, fine branded horses, cattle and tilled land. That is the enjoyment of worldly life, but God has with Him the best return [that is, paradise]. Say, "Shall I inform you of something better than that? For those who fear God will be gardens beneath which rivers flow, wherein they abide eternally, and purified spouses and approval from God..."

(Qur'aan 3:14-15)

Therefore, the real competition in this life is not the accumulation of wealth or the desire for fame; it is racing with one another to perform good deeds to please God, while having our lawful portion of enjoyment in this life.

XIV THE RIGHT PATH TO GOD

There are many religious alternatives available to man and it is up to him to choose the one he wishes to follow. He is like a merchant with many goods in front of him, and it is his choice which one to trade in. He will obviously select the one he thinks will be the most lucrative. However, the merchant is unsure and has no guarantee of prosperity; his product may have a market and he may make handsome returns, but he could just as easily lose all of his money. In contrast, the believer in the oneness of God who submits to His will as a Muslim, is completely sure that if he follows the path of guidance — the Qur'aan and the Sunnah of Prophet Muhammad, there will undoubtedly be success and reward waiting for him at the end of this path. Fortunately, this success also starts at the beginning of the path.

Aboo Sa'eed al-Khudree (may God be pleased with him) narrated that God's Messenger (peace be upon him) said,

"If a person embraces Islam sincerely, then God shall forgive all his past sins. After that, starts the settlement of accounts: the reward of his good deeds will be greater in value by ten to seven hundred times, and an evil deed will be recorded as it is unless God forgives it."

EPILOGUE

Based on my search for the truth, I concluded that the precise way we believe in God and the deeds we perform determine our future condition for eternity. Our Creator is giving us all an equal chance, regardless of our circumstances, to earn His pleasure in preparation for Judgment Day, as in the following Qur'anic verses:

وَأَطِيعُوا۟ ٱللَّهَ وَٱلرَّسُولَ لَعَلَّكُمْ تُرْحَمُونَ ۝ ۞ وَسَارِعُوٓا۟ إِلَىٰ مَغْفِرَةٍ مِّن رَّبِّكُمْ وَجَنَّةٍ عَرْضُهَا ٱلسَّمَٰوَٰتُ وَٱلْأَرْضُ أُعِدَّتْ لِلْمُتَّقِينَ ۝

"Obey God and His messenger that you may obtain mercy. And hasten to forgiveness from your Lord and a garden [that is, paradise] as wide as the heavens and earth, prepared for the righteous."

(Qur'aan 3:132-133)

If we sincerely seek the truth of this life, which is Islam (peaceful submission to the will of God), God will guide us there, God willing. He directs us to examine the life and the Sunnah of Prophet Muhammad, as *he* is the best role model for mankind to follow.

Furthermore, God directs us to investigate and ponder what He says in the Qur'aan. One will see that the Qur'aan is indeed like a persistent and strong knocking on a door, or loud shouts seeking to awaken those who are fast asleep because they are just completely absorbed by this life on earth. The knocks and shouts appear one after the other: Wake up! Look around you! Think! Reflect! God is there! There is planning, trial, accountability, reckoning, reward, severe punishment and lasting bliss!

Clearly and unequivocally, the *best* way to live and die in this world, is as a righteous Muslim! When one comes to the conclusion that Islam is the truth, he should not delay in becoming a Muslim because he may die first, and then — it will be too late.

A few months after embracing Islam, I found two verses in the Qur'aan that mirror what the American Muslim told me regarding how we should live and die:

وَوَصَّىٰ بِهَآ إِبْرَٰهِۦمُ بَنِيهِ وَيَعْقُوبُ يَٰبَنِيَّ إِنَّ ٱللَّهَ ٱصْطَفَىٰ لَكُمُ ٱلدِّينَ فَلَا تَمُوتُنَّ إِلَّا وَأَنتُم مُّسْلِمُونَ ﴿١٣٢﴾

"Abraham instructed his sons and so did Jacob, saying, "My sons, indeed God has chosen for you this religion, so do not die except while you are Muslims."

(Qur'aan 2:132)

يَٰٓأَيُّهَا ٱلَّذِينَ ءَامَنُوا۟ ٱتَّقُوا۟ ٱللَّهَ حَقَّ تُقَاتِهِۦ وَلَا تَمُوتُنَّ إِلَّا وَأَنتُم مُّسْلِمُونَ ﴿١٠٢﴾

"O you who have believed, fear God as He *should* be feared and do not die, except as Muslims in submission to Him."

(Qur'aan 3:102)

90